Be Careful What You Wish For!

Mick Gowar
Illustrated by Keri Rosebraugh

Rigby®

A Harcourt Achieve Imprint

www.Rigby.com
1-800-531-5015

Literacy by Design Leveled Readers: *Be Careful What You Wish For!*

ISBN-13: 978-1-4189-3917-5
ISBN-10:   1-4189-3917-X

Printed in China
1B 2 3 4 5 6 7 8 985 13 12 11 10 09 08 07

Contents

The Fisherman's Tale

Chapter 1 5
Chapter 2 13
Chapter 3 19
Chapter 4 23
Chapter 5 28

The Magical Pasta Pot

Chapter 1 36
Chapter 2 40
Chapter 3 47
Chapter 4 52

The Fisherman's Tale
Chapter 1

"I'm fed up!" shouted the fisherman's wife, looking at her husband across the table. "Look at this place! The rain drips through the holes in the roof, and the wind whistles through the cracks in the walls." She banged her spoon on the table, which wobbled, and some thin, watery porridge slopped out of the pot.

"Bella, my little rosebud," said her husband in a soothing voice. "Don't get so upset. We have a good life together—don't we?"

"Aaargh!" shouted Bella, and she plunged the spoon into the pot, scooped up some porridge, and slopped it into her bowl. "My mother was right! I should never have married you. I should have married Luigi, the butcher. He and Maria live in the finest house in the village. Maria always has new clothes and the most beautiful shoes. They eat the finest beef and the plumpest chickens. They have a cook and a gardener. We don't even have a donkey to carry our water and firewood. Oh, Fredo, Fredo!" She burst into tears.

Fredo put his arms around his wife. "Don't be sad, my sweet, sweet flower," he said. "We may not be rich, but at least we're happy—aren't we?"

"Happy? You might be, but I am not!" wailed Bella, wiping her eyes. "Life wouldn't be so bad if you were a good fisherman, Fredo, but you're terrible."

"I try my best, darling Bella," said Fredo, "but a fisherman needs luck, and I have very little of it."

"When was the last time you caught anything?" demanded Bella.

Fredo stared at the ceiling and tried to think.

"Aaargh! I'll tell you!" shouted Bella. "It was two weeks ago. Fredo, we should be eating trout and salmon every day! We should be eating shrimp and lobster!"

She pointed at the pot on the table. "Instead, we're eating this disgusting porridge! Sometimes I think you don't actually go fishing at all. I think you just sit on the shore of the lake all day, staring up at the clouds."

"No, no," said Fredo. "Each day I fish until my fingers ache and my arms are stiff. It's just bad luck when I don't catch anything. But today, my blossom . . . today will be different! I can feel it."

"Humph!" snorted Bella. "That's what you said yesterday, and the day before that, and the day before that! In fact, that's what you say *every* day!"

"But I know today will be different," Fredo said softly as he buttoned up his coat and gathered up his rod, net, and lunch sack. "Today my luck will change, and tonight we will feast upon the greatest catch any fisherman has ever caught!" He closed the door behind him and heard Bella grumbling from inside the hut.

Fredo strode down the steep path toward the lake, whistling, happy to feel the sun on his back. From deep in the woods beside the path came the call of a woodpecker—*chur-chur-chur*—followed by the sharp *rat-a-tat* of its beak tapping a tree trunk.

When Fredo reached the shore of the lake, he looked out across the sparkling water at the snow-capped mountains in the distance. This was his favorite spot in the whole world.

He chose a smooth, round rock, sat down on it, and carefully prepared his fishing line. He then cast his baited hook out into the water, and lay back against his rock to watch the clouds skim slowly across the sky.

Just as Fredo was drifting off to sleep in the warm morning sun, he heard a loud splash. He sat up and wondered if he might have caught something. He pulled his line from the water, but his hook was empty.

Then Fredo spotted a brown, furry head with small round ears breaking the water's surface. It was an otter. The creature rolled onto its back and began to gnaw at a small fish it was gripping between its paws.

Fredo sighed. Looking up at the sun, he decided it was time for lunch. He reached into his sack and pulled out a small hunk of dry bread and a bottle of apple juice. "I'm not a very good fisherman, but at least I can enjoy my lunch beside this beautiful lake," he thought to himself as he drank from his bottle of juice.

Chapter 2

As his wife had suspected, Fredo spent most of the afternoon dozing or watching the birds and animals of the lake. Only when the clouds began to change color and the cool, late-afternoon breeze began to blow across the lake did he remember to check his fishing line. He reeled it in and lifted up the hook, but the bait had all been nibbled away.

"Bella's right," thought Fredo, ashamed. "I am a hopeless fisherman. But what else can I do? If I were a butcher or a baker or a bank clerk, I'd never be able to enjoy all of this beauty. Working in a shop or in an office all day would seem like prison."

He sighed.

Fredo stood and gathered his fishing gear. "I suppose I *should* try harder to catch a fish, for poor Bella's sake." He walked a little way along the shore to a point where a small stream flowed into the lake. He climbed down to the end of a small rocky point and cast his line once again into the clear water.

The float had barely settled on the water's surface when there was a sharp tug on the line. It had been so long since Fredo had felt a bite that he didn't quite believe he had one now.

After another sharp tug, though, Fredo quickly reeled the line in, his rod bent almost

in two under the weight of a truly enormous fish. Fredo struggled to bring the fish into the shallows, then scooped it out of the water with his net.

"Oh!" cried the fish. "Please let me go!"

Fredo was so astonished that he dropped the net, fish and all, onto the sandy lakeshore.

"Ouch!" yelped the fish. "That hurt—nearly as much as that horrible hook in my lip. Would you kindly remove it before you let me go?"

Fredo blinked repeatedly and rubbed his eyes. "A talking fish! Amazing! Wait till I show it to my Bella," he whispered to himself as he gently removed the sharp hook from the fish's mouth.

"Bella?" said the fish. "Who's Bella?"

"Bella is my wife," replied Fredo. "She's always telling me that I'm not a very good fisherman, but when she sees you, she'll certainly change her mind. Not only can you talk, but you are the most beautiful fish I've ever seen!"

It was true—the fish was breathtaking. Its body shimmered gold and emerald in the evening sunlight, its fins shone like pieces of silver, and its eyes were huge sparkling discs flecked with scarlet.

"You're not really going to take me away from the lake, are you?" gasped the fish.

"I won't hurt you," said Fredo. "I'm going to put you in a big glass tank, and people will pay to see you," said Fredo.

"Oh, please don't do that!" begged the fish. "I wouldn't last a week cooped up in a tank. My place is here in the lake with the other fish. How would you like to be trapped in a glass tank for the rest of your life, away from the lake and the sunlight?"

Fredo gazed out over the lake, thinking about what the fish had said.

"Please set me free!" the fish continued. "I'll be your friend, I promise. I'm very clever—I'm a talking fish, after all—and you never know when you might need my help."

Fredo sighed. "I don't know how you could ever help me, but I know how I would feel if I were taken away from the lake and forced to live in a tank."

And with that, he put the fish back into the water and watched it swim away. The beautiful fish sped off toward the middle of the lake, slowed down, then turned back and swam toward Fredo again.

"Thank you, thank you so much for setting me free!" cried the fish. "If you ever need my help, you only have to ask me."

"How would I do that?" asked Fredo.

"Just place a silver coin in your net and dip the net into the lake. I'll know it's you."

Then the beautiful fish leaped high into the air, flashed its tail in the setting sun, dived deeply back into the water, and vanished.

Fredo again rubbed his eyes. Then he slowly set off for home, shaking his head in amazement.

Chapter 3

"You did WHAT?" shouted Fredo's wife.

"I let it go," replied Fredo. "The poor fish pleaded so sadly, what else could I do?"

"You have no brains at all—not a single cell!" roared Bella. "Have you never read a folktale, not even when you were small? Talking frogs, talking fish, *any* talking animals—what do they always give to the people who catch them?"

"I have no idea," answered Fredo. "I was never a great one for reading. I always preferred being out in the fresh air, walking, or climbing, or . . . "

"Aaargh! Or staring at the clouds and daydreaming! Talking animals always grant three wishes," explained Bella.

"Do they?" Fredo asked.

"Of course they do!" Bella shouted. "Now go back and tell that fish to grant yours!"

In the faint light of dawn, Fredo stood beside the lakeshore. He carefully placed his only silver coin in the bottom of his net and lowered it into the water. Almost at once he felt the net get heavy.

"Good morning," said the fish cheerfully. "You're up quite early."

Fredo cleared his throat and tried to remember what Bella had told him to say:

"I've caught you in my net, O fish,
And won't set you free till I have my wish."

The fish narrowed its eyes suspiciously. "Whom have you been talking to?"

"What do you mean?" replied Fredo.

"What's with all the rhyming speech business?" asked the fish.

"Oh, that was Bella's idea," said Fredo.

"Uh-huh. So you want a wish, do you?" asked the fish. "Don't tell me, let me take a guess—a big house, buckets of money, fine new clothes—am I right?"

"Yes!" said Fredo. "How did you know? You *are* a magic fish!"

The fish shook its head sadly. "That's what all humans wish for. Frankly, I was expecting something a little more original from you."

"Well, to be perfectly honest," confided Fredo, "that was Bella's idea, too. I'm quite happy with our life, but she wants a bigger house than Luigi the butcher and his wife, Maria, and new shoes, and . . . "

The fish sighed. "So Bella wants to be a wealthy lady, hmm?"

Fredo nodded.

"All right, then," said the fish. "I will grant your wish. But I warn you, you're not going to like it."

"Why do you say that?" Fredo asked.

"Because whatever I do, it won't be enough to please Bella," answered the fish. "You'll see."

Chapter 4

Fredo sat in his chair, staring out the window. He could just barely see the lake far in the distance, the blue water glistening in the sunlight. He sighed. He did not like these long days, shut inside the huge house with nothing to do. He wanted to be beside the lake fishing or watching the birds or clouds. But Bella wouldn't allow it. "Fine ladies and gentlemen don't go fishing," she had told him.

Suddenly, Fredo's peace was broken by a loud shout. All the windowpanes trembled.

"Fredo! Where are you?" bellowed Bella.

"I'm here, my lovely snowflake," he called, "in the library."

In rushed Bella. "The library? Why are you wasting time in here? You don't read!"

"Whatever is the matter, my sugarplum?" asked Fredo.

"What's the matter? I'll tell you what the matter is!" snapped Bella impatiently. "It's that worthless stable boy, Marco. He spends all day in the kitchen chatting with the maids, and when I tell him to do his work, he just laughs at me. And I heard him whispering about me under his breath."

"What should I do?" asked Fredo.

"Fire him!" shouted Bella. "Throw him out! I won't have him in this house one minute longer!"

"But you've had me fire two maids, a cook, and three gardeners this week already," said Fredo.

"They don't respect me," wailed Bella. "They call me rude names behind my back, and they won't do as they are told. Oh, I'm so unhappy!" She burst into tears.

Fredo put his arms round her. "Don't be sad, my cupcake," he said.

"Go back to that fish right now and make another wish!" demanded Bella.

"Yes, of course!" said Fredo, grinning broadly. "I'll ask him to take away all the maids and cooks and gardeners and—"

"Noooooo!" wailed Bella. "I don't want to get rid of all of them. What would Luigi and Maria think? I just want them all to respect and obey me."

Fredo stood with his mouth open. "How do I wish for that?" he asked.

"Tell the fish to make me a princess!" declared Bella. "Then everyone will have to respect me—even Luigi and that proud wife of his. I want an even larger house, and guards on horseback to salute me."

"Are you sure, my little pumpkin?" Fredo asked.

"NOW!" Bella replied.

Fredo set off for the lake. As he walked down the path, he realized how much he missed the woods and the birds. The warm sun and the scented air made Fredo feel happy for the first time in weeks.

He whistled as he approached the water's edge. He pulled a silver coin from his pocket, dropped it into the net, and dipped the net into the cool water. At once, Fredo felt the net sag with the weight of the fish.

"I've caught you in my net, O fish–"

"Ah!" interrupted the fish. "I've been expecting you. And you can skip all that nonsense."

"I'm sorry to trouble you," said Fredo, "but Bella is so unhappy. She asked me to catch you and make another wish."

The fish groaned and rolled its shining eyes. "What does she want this time?"

"She wants to be a princess, in a bigger house, with guards on horseback," said the weary Fredo.

"I wouldn't recommend it, you know. Honestly, she'll hate it. You'll hate it, too. It's not what you think it is," said the fish.

Fredo shook his head. "Bella wants to be a princess."

"All right, if you insist," said the fish. "But don't say I didn't warn you."

And with that, Bella became a princess.

Chapter 5

CRASH!

The chandelier fell from the ceiling, bringing down a huge chunk of plaster and smashing into a thousand tinkling pieces. Fredo crawled under the table for cover. The maids and stable boys and cooks and guards were having a big party, and things had gotten a little out of control.

"Bella!" Fredo cried out. "What's happening? Where are you?"

There was brief silence. Then Fredo heard a door slam, followed by laughter. He scampered out from under the table just in time to see the parlor maids, dressed in Bella's finest gowns, running across the lawn outside. As he looked out the window, he saw

the stable boys mounted on the princess's white horses, galloping across the gardens and churning up all the flowers.

Fredo flung open the library door and called out, "Bella, can you hear me?"

"I'm in here. Of course I can hear you!" came an angry voice from the kitchen.

Fredo found his wife sitting in the middle of the kitchen floor. Food and smashed dishes lay everywhere.

Bella sobbed, "They're all impossible! The maids won't do anything I say, and they torment me with rudeness. The stable boys say I'm not worthy to be a princess!"

"But Bella, you are *my* princess," soothed Fredo. "How can I make it all better?"

"*Better? Better?* It's all your fault! You are the reason things are so awful! Go find that fish and fix things, NOW!"

At the lakeshore, the fish said, "I'll bet she wants to be queen now, right?"

"Yes! Oh, you're so clever, fish! I knew you could fix things!" Fredo exclaimed.

"You just don't get it, do you?" asked the fish. "OK, but this is it. It's your third wish, and everybody knows you only get three."

"Thank you, oh, thank you, fish!"

Fredo returned home to find that the huge house was now a palace. Hundreds of maids and guards were having cake and punch in the great hall. Dirty plates and cups were scattered everywhere. There was so much music and laughter and noise that, at first, Fredo couldn't hear the loud barking coming from upstairs. When he finally did hear it, he ran up the sweeping staircase to look for his wife, shouting, "Bella, Bella, my queen!"

Fredo found his wife on top of a huge wardrobe. Hunting dogs snarled and snapped at her. "Bella!" he wailed.

"Don't you 'Bella' me! This is your fault. It's always your fault! Do something with these dogs and get me down, NOW!"

Once Fredo had rescued his wife, he stood with his head bowed as she spoke.

"You are useless! You were useless as a fisherman, and you're even more useless as a maker of wishes! I suppose I'm going to have to take care of things myself, as usual!" she complained.

"But Bella, my lollipop, I've already used all my wishes!"

"*Your* wishes, yes, but every person gets three. Don't you know anything?" his wife cried.

Beside the lake, Bella demanded, "Give me the net."

Fredo handed her the net and placed a silver coin in it. "I'm not so sure—"

"Quiet!" Bella shouted. "I thought you said the fish would just come if I lowered the net into the water."

"Hello," said a pleasant, fishy voice. "And who might this be?"

"Oh, hello, fish. This is Bella," Fredo answered. The fish swam in circles a small distance from the net.

"Hello, Queen Bella," the fish said.

"Don't you 'hello' me, you fish! I demand my three wishes!"

"Demand, is it? We're a little pushy, aren't we?"

"Aaargh!" Bella shouted. "I wish I could get my hands on you—"

SPLASH!

Bella found herself in the lake! She thrashed about, struggling to keep her head above water. She coughed and sputtered, paddling with her left hand and kicking her stubby legs. In her right hand she held . . . the talking fish!

"Oh! I wish I were a better swimmer!" Bella moaned. And suddenly, staying afloat was no longer a struggle. Bella released the fish and swam easily to shore. She hauled herself up out of the water and stood, soaked and dripping, on the sand.

"Bella, my tulip, you're safe!" Fredo cried. He threw his arms around his soggy wife.

"Oh, Fredo, Fredo," Bella declared, "I wish you had never caught that fish in the first place."

FOOM! The sky instantly brightened. A gentle breeze carried the scent of spring flowers and the soft chirping of happy birds. Fredo and Bella looked down at themselves. Their fine, dripping clothes had disappeared, and they were now dressed like a poor fisherman and his wife. The surface of the lake was as smooth as glass, and there was no sign of the beautiful fish anywhere. Fredo offered his hand to his wife, and she gladly took it in her own.

Back in their leaky hut, as they sat down to supper in welcome peace and quiet, Fredo asked, "We are happy, aren't we, my lovely sweet pea?"

Bella sighed, and for the first time in a very, very long time, she smiled. "Yes," she told her husband. "Yes, Fredo, we really are quite happy."

And watery porridge never tasted so good.

The Magical Pasta Pot
Chapter 1

Across the lake from where the fisherman lived, high up on the steep mountainside, was an ancient village. In a tiny cottage on the edge of the village lived Carla, an old woman who was well known as the greatest pasta cook in the whole region.

Once, many years before, the winter had been very harsh. The snow began to fall in December and didn't stop falling until February. The village children loved the snow. The younger children made snowmen, while the older children built a giant snow fort on the playground. But the grownups disliked the snow. They struggled to haul their sleds full of firewood down from the pine forests, along paths that had all but disappeared.

Even after the snow stopped, the air remained bitterly cold. The wells had frozen solid and the streets were covered with ice. Icicles hung from every building like long, frosty fingers.

It was the last week of February when old Carla slipped on the icy cobblestones as she was coming out of the bakery. She fell hard, twisting her ankle and crying out in pain. Villagers gathered around her, and Gino, the baker's son, was sent to find old Santino and his donkey.

Santino and his skinny donkey—the most sure-footed creature in the village—soon arrived, and together they carried old Carla down the icy mountainside to the town at the base of the peak. They took her to see the only doctor for miles around.

"I'm afraid that's a nasty sprain," the doctor said. "You can't put any weight on your ankle for two weeks."

"But how will I gather firewood or shop for food?"

"Is there someone who could come and stay with you?" asked the doctor.

"There's my grandson, Alberto. He comes to visit every spring, when the snow thaws."

"Well," said the doctor, "it looks like he may need to come a bit earlier."

Chapter 2

Old Santino took a message to Carla's daughter, and in a few days Alberto arrived to look after his grandmother. He worked hard for her. Every day he set off for the shops and the market, and he returned huffing and puffing, carrying heavy sacks. He dragged firewood down from the forest and carried water from the only working well.

The village children were curious about Alberto. They thought it was funny that he had to work so hard while they played all day in the snow.

"Alberto! You work like a donkey!" the noisy Bruno shouted as Alberto struggled on the icy steps, bent over under a heavy sack of potatoes.

"I'm back, Grandmother," Alberto called as he pushed open the door.

41

He dragged the heavy sack of potatoes into the kitchen and put some dry pasta in a pot. As he lit the stove, his grandmother called from the bedroom.

"Alberto, will you bring me a lantern?"

Alberto set the pot onto the stove and ran to fetch a lantern. "Light it, will you, so I can see to read," old Carla asked. "And bring me my reading glasses."

Alberto lit the lantern, added wood to the fire, and went to find his grandmother's glasses. He moved slowly, for he was tired from all the fetching and hauling.

"What's that smell?" asked old Carla as Alberto handed her the glasses. "Something is burning. Alberto, there is smoke coming from the kitchen!"

Oh, no! Alberto rushed to the kitchen to find smoke pouring from the pot on the stove. "Ohhh!" the boy groaned. He opened the back door and dumped the smoldering pasta into the deep snow.

"What? What?" demanded old Carla in alarm.

"It was the pasta, Grandmother," said Alberto. "I forgot to put any water in the pot before I lit the stove."

"Foolish boy," said the old woman. "You know I'm the best pasta cook in the village. Move out of my way. "

"But how can you possibly cook dinner, Grandmother? You can't even walk," protested Alberto.

"I don't need to walk," replied Carla. "Just bring me the pasta pot, the old iron one on the shelf, and place it on the table." Alberto did as he was told. "Now," said his grandmother, "you must promise never to tell anyone what you are about to see and hear—do you understand?"

Alberto nodded.

Old Carla closed her eyes, placed her hands on the lid of the pot, and said in a quiet voice:

"Old friend, old faithful pot,
Please cook me pasta, piping hot."

Alberto's mouth fell open as the pot began to steam and bubble. In seconds the pot was filled with freshly cooked pasta. "Don't stand there with your mouth open, boy!" Carla said with a grin. "You know your grandmother is the best pasta cook in the village."

A knock came at the door.

"Answer it, Alberto," whispered Carla, "but don't let anyone in. No one must see my pasta pot!"

As Alberto walked to the door, he could hear his grandmother whispering quietly, but he couldn't tell what she was saying.

On the porch was old Santino. His skinny donkey stood in the yard.

"I've come to see if your grandmother needs me to take her to the doctor."

"I'm sorry, but she can't see anyone," said Alberto. "She's resting."

"Who is it?" called Carla.

"It's Santino," replied Alberto.

"Well, don't keep him standing outside in this cold weather," shouted Carla. "Let him in, foolish boy!"

Alberto did as he was told. The pot had stopped bubbling, and it stood on the table, filled with delicious, steaming pasta.

"Come in, Santino," said Carla. "I've just cooked supper—you must eat with us. I may have hurt my ankle, but I'm still the best pasta cook in the whole village!"

As they ate in silence, Alberto thought to himself, "It's not you who is the great pasta cook, Grandmother. It's your magical pot!"

Chapter 3

The next day Carla had to return to the doctor. "Now don't forget, Alberto," the old woman said, handing the boy a long list as Santino lifted her onto his donkey. "Buy our meat from the market, not from Luigi the butcher. He's too expensive, and his meat's not fresh. And be sure to get white turnips this time—the yellow ones taste awful. I'll be home before dark."

Alberto entered the village, slipping and sliding along the icy path. It took all morning to buy everything his grandmother had asked for. As he struggled back up the hill, he heard a voice call out, "Hey! Alberto! *Heeee-haw!*"

Alberto turned. "Leave me alone!" he shouted.

"*Heee-haw!*" chanted Bruno. "*Heee-haw!*"

"I'm no donkey," shouted Alberto. "I'm not, I tell you! I'm . . . I'm . . . I'm the greatest pasta cook in the country!"

The children stopped chanting.

"Oh, yes?" said Bruno. "The greatest pasta cook in the country? All right then. Show us!"

Bruno and several other children followed Alberto up the hill to old Carla's cottage.

"Wait here," said Alberto. "It will take me a few seconds."

"You can't make pasta in a few seconds," said Bruno, puzzled.

"I can!" replied Alberto, bragging once more.

Alone in the kitchen, he took the old iron pasta pot from the shelf and set it on the floor. He closed his eyes and placed his hands on the lid, just as he'd seen his grandmother do. Then he whispered:

"Old friend, old faithful pot,
Please cook me pasta, piping hot."

Sure enough, the pot began to steam and bubble, and soon the kitchen was filled with the delicious smell of fresh pasta. Bruno burst into the kitchen, followed by the other children.

"Whoa!" said Bruno. "It's true! You must be the greatest pasta cook in the country! Even my mother can't make supper that quickly!"

Alberto stared anxiously at the pot. The pasta was beginning to push the lid off.

"Out of my kitchen!" cried Alberto. "I must add my special, secret ingredient! Out! Out!"

The children ran out. Alberto closed his eyes, pressed his hands down over the lid, and cried, "Stop, pot!" He opened his eyes, but the spaghetti was now spilling out of the pot onto the floor. Alberto shut his eyes again and sat on the lid this time, shouting, "That's enough, please, pot! Stop!"

Spaghetti flooded across the kitchen floor. Soon it was flowing under the door and into the other rooms of the cottage.

"Please! Please! Nice pasta pot, beautiful pasta pot—please STOP!"

Moments later, Santino and his donkey, with old Carla perched on the saddle, turned the corner into the village and saw a huge wave of pasta oozing down the center of the street. Floating along on top of the wave were several village children, including Alberto and Bruno, who both clutched the pot from which pasta continued to pour.

"Oh, no!" groaned old Carla. "Alberto! You foolish, foolish boy!"

She closed her eyes, stretched out her arms and said:

"Old friend, old faithful pot,
Thank you for pasta, piping hot."

The pot stopped bubbling. Lowering herself from the donkey, the old woman grabbed the pot away from her grandson

Alberto blushed. "Please forgive me, Grandmother! I just wanted the children to stop teasing me and calling me a donkey."

"You're as foolish as a donkey!" Carla said. "You show-off! All you had to do was be polite and say thank you! Now the whole village knows my secret. Take me home."

Chapter 4

Alberto helped his grandmother into her chair, lit the fire, and fetched her a hot cup of turnip soup. Neither of them spoke a word.

Alberto had revealed his grandmother's secret. Now the whole village knew that it was the magical pot—not old Carla—that made the most delicious pasta in the village.

There came another knock on the door. Alberto looked fearfully at his grandmother. She slowly lifted her head from her book and said, "Go and answer it, foolish Alberto!"

With a pounding heart Alberto opened the door. On the porch stood Santino. All the other villagers were on the path behind him.

"Who is it?" asked Carla.

"It's . . . it's . . . everyone," Alberto said nervously.

"What?" snorted old Carla. "Come to tease you, foolish boy, and it would serve you right!"

"No, we haven't come to tease Alberto," Santino said. "We've come to thank him."

"Thank him!" said Carla. "What have you to thank him for?"

"Well," said Santino, "he provided the entire village with the most delicious pasta anyone has ever tasted. And what's more, the hot pasta melted away all the snow and ice, so the village streets are safe again! People can get to work and school without hurting themselves."

Carla looked at her grandson, and a smile slowly crept over her wrinkled face.

"Well, Alberto," she said, "it looks like all is well." She pinched her grandson's cheek, then turned to Santino and the others. "Alberto and I were about to have supper," she said. "Would anyone care to join us?"

"Er . . . well, that's very kind of you," said the mayor.

"But you see . . . " said the schoolteacher.

"What we're trying to say," interrupted the baker, "is that as wonderful as your pasta is, we've eaten so much that we couldn't swallow another bite of it."

"Ah!" exclaimed Carla. "Then you're in luck. Alberto and I were going to have rice for supper!"

The villagers crowded into Carla's small cottage while Alberto helped his grandmother in the kitchen.

"Grandmother!" protested Alberto. "We don't have nearly enough rice to feed all of these people."

"Pass me down that old rice pan—the one on the top shelf," said the old woman, ignoring her grandson. "And promise me two things: you'll never show off again . . . "

"I promise!" said Alberto.

" . . . and you will never, ever, breathe a word of what you are about to see!"